Strannik

Other books by Catherine de Hueck Doherty:

POUSTINIA

THE GOSPEL WITHOUT COMPROMISE

NOT WITHOUT PARABLES

SOBORNOST

Strannik

The Call to Pilgrimage for Western Man

Catherine de Hueck Doherty

AVE MARIA PRESS
Notre Dame, Indiana 46556

Library of Congress Catalog Card Number: 78-58212

International Standard Book Number: 0-87793-155-0 (Paper)
0-87793-156-9 (Cloth)

© 1978 by Ave Maria Press, Notre Dame, Indiana 46556

Cover photo: Billy Barnes
Art: Carolyn Desch

Printed and bound in the United States of America.

Contents

1. The Remembrance of Paradise

STRANNIK IS THE RUSSIAN WORD for "pilgrim," and this book is about pilgrims and pilgrimages.

It seems to me that a book on pilgrimage has to be written. Somehow, deep in my heart, I know that I should write it because the pilgrimages I want to speak about are not made on beautiful ships with all the slick conveniences of modern travel, or on planes that bring you quickly from one place to another. No. The pilgrimage I want to talk about is the life-pilgrimage.

It is rather obvious, of course, to everyone, that life is a pilgrimage. The expression, "Life is a pilgrimage," has been used and abused over and over again. But what is a pilgrimage? God, evidently, loves pilgrims. To some, like Tobias, he sent angels as guides. To others, like Abraham, he just said, "Arise and go." Abraham could be called one of the first pilgrims.

I wonder what happened to Adam and Eve when they left the Garden? They had been told to look after and cherish it and yet they were taken out of paradise just the same. They didn't know it, but they had been given another paradise. It is quite evident that they must have embarked on a pilgrimage. Above all, Adam and Eve embarked on a pilgrimage with *a nostalgia for what had been. The audible, visible presence of God, his friendship, was like a fire, or must have been, in the hearts of Adam and Eve!* Were they nomads? Were they hunters? Did they know about sowing and harvesting? It's not really important. They were pilgrims. They were the first pilgrims of the Absolute because they had known the Absolute. Yes, they had known the Absolute and this knowledge passed into all their children's hearts.

Millions upon millions have been pilgrims in India, in lost civilizations, in Christian times and in our times. The fire was something that could not be quenched, something that could not be killed, something hidden in a corner of man's heart. Few followed its call, but some did. Some did, and the history of mankind is filled with those who "arose and left all things." To follow what? To follow whom? A reality? Who can say?

Consider the prophets. They were told to "arise and go," but that was because from their very childhood they had a dream, a dream of seeking the Absolute. Oh, they tried to squash it, to quench it, to deny it, but they couldn't. The Absolute called to them. Out of some depth unknown to them they heard that voice. They may not have seen— some I think did; they may not have seen him who called, but yet they knew. They knew who it was who called and they couldn't resist. They had to arise. They had to go out of big cities, out of beautiful surroundings, out of rich houses with soft and downy couches, away from wine, song and carnal attractions. They had to go. They had to go and nothing could hold them back.

Neither relatives, nor pressure groups, nor businesses, nor anything human restrained them, for always those pilgrims had a strange way of listening. Why do I imagine that their heads were always a little to the side as if they were trying to catch a voice that was indistinct? They were making sure, as it were, that they heard it. And hearing, they arose. Half the time they didn't know where they were going, and many in the beginning didn't even know why. But this persistent strange voice, that was no voice at all, spoke distinctly, though it wasn't audible.

Yes, the nostalgia. No, that's not the word at all. It was the *hunger* that Adam and Eve experienced when they had to leave the friendship of God, the vision of God. This hunger came to them at eventide—a hunger for friendship, for oneness with God. That was what they cried out for. That was what the banishment was all about.

I am no theologian. I don't know if there were angels standing with swords—I feel sure there were—but I can just see the scene. I can see Adam and Eve standing outside the gates of what we call "paradise" for lack of any other word. There are thousands of paradises on earth too, but this was something special because it was a place. It had to be a place because Adam and Eve were human, and their humanness consisted in the unity of God, man and woman.

Just think of it: the *sobornost** of the Trinity penetrated, became incarnate in the sobornost of the man and the woman. And then, by some sort of incredible miracle, the sobornost of the Trinity and the sobornost of man, as represented by Adam and Eve, were one. It's beyond understanding, so let us bow low before this mystery.

No wonder that this moment somehow was captured for all eternity in the hearts of all men. They dreamt strange dreams of that unity, that sobornost. Some spoke of their dreams and were called sorcerers and heretics. But they were not. They did not give the apple to Eve. They were not Christians who knew that God is the Lord of History and that he touches everybody. They were people

---

*Russian word for "unity." The book, *Sobornost*, was published by Ave Maria Press, 1977.

such as the Three Kings, or the little two-by-four Papua in
the desert of Australia, or the tall, seven-foot African. All
men who have religion of some sort are dreamers, and
dreamers of a very special kind. They dream of unity with
God, and men in total sobornost (unity). It is the dream
conferred upon, handed over as a treasure to Adam and
Eve. Men can develop that dream or let it lie unrecalled.

Yes. Sobornost! When all is said and done, what is
man really seeking? Obviously he is often moved by the
pleasure principle, though the pain principle is built into
him too, as it is in animals. But deep down, hidden under
all kinds of emotional fears, lies the hidden dream of unity,
of oneness with the God of all creation.

Perhaps it isn't a dream at all. Perhaps it is a remembrance, and the word "pilgrimage" in every language
refers to the remembrance. Then the remembrance
becomes a dream, and, for some, a reality. Pilgrims have
to leave everything behind, I repeat, and follow this reality
that is hidden in the mist of time.

Who is to explain the migration of peoples all over
the world? Back and forth, back and forth. They didn't
move simply because they were nomads or farmers, though
that might be part of it. But I believe that in the collective
hearts of all those tribes there was hidden the gift that
Adam and Eve left to all of us: unity with God. Sobornost!

Angry because their dream never reached reality as
they expected it to do, they built Towers of Babel to reach
God, or they fought among themselves in sheer anger for
the possession of this or that piece of land. Officially the
conflict was for political, economical or cultural reasons.
But is it possible for one Russian in love with God to say
without fear and trembling that perhaps all this was done
and is still being done in pursuit of Adam and Eve's
heritage?

For the hunger for God is growing in leaps and bounds all across the world, and it is still visible, palpable in the Third World, whatever beliefs of its people may be. Could it all be in pursuit of a dream that is a reality, the only true reality that exists?

Well, all I can say is what comes to me in the dark of the nights like a light: this might be the crying of humanity to God.

I have written a book called *Poustinia** in which, in a manner of speaking, I tried to meet the need for prayer. "Poustinia" is the Russian word for "desert," and a poustinia may be a room, a shack, or one's own heart. But before one enters into the poustinia one must understand what sobornost is: unity among ourselves—all peoples, all nations—and God.

It is on unity, on sobornost, that we meditate in the poustinia. It is for sobornost, for this unity, that we pray in the poustinia. For we were created to be one with God as in "paradise." That unity was restored upon Christ's arrival, Christ's Incarnation.

Christ was the total pilgrim, the man who pilgrimaged from the bosom of his Father to the hearts of men. Christ, who lived among men as men do. Christ, who became the bridge between all men and God. Christ, who died for all men, no matter who they were, sinners or saints, Hindus or Arabs.

He is the Lord of History. He is the bridge between the Father and men. He invites us to a pilgrimage, the supreme pilgrimage. He offers himself as *the* path. "I am the way," he said, "to the Father." You can call him "the way." Christ offered himself—the path, the way—to the Father, giving us the opportunity to become one with the

---

*Ave Maria Press, 1975.

Father again, one with himself, and with the Holy Spirit. To be one, with God. To know God as Adam and Eve knew him.

Yes, Christ was the Supreme Pilgrim, the incredible pilgrim who descended from heaven to earth and returned from earth to heaven, thereby making us free. Free to love and free to serve. Free to undertake a pilgrimage of that love. There is no denying that every Christian, of course, must make a pilgrimage of love. He enters into the pilgrimage of love to the Father, to God. He has to love his neighbor. It is a long pilgrimage, because he has to love himself before he can love anybody else. He has to walk that long road inward, take that journey, that pilgrimage inward that alone will make him touch Christ who dwells within.

There is another part to the pilgrimage. Namely, the pilgrim must love those who hate him and be good to those who are not good to him, even to the point of giving away his clothing and his belongings. And finally he has to enter into the pilgrimage of fire.

There is a pilgrimage of fire since Christ came. Some completed that pilgrimage, and some didn't, but the dream was in their hearts.

There is always offered now this pilgrimage of fire. It is a pilgrimage of passionate, incredible love that would give itself to be a path for Christ to walk on. To lay our life down for another is to make a red carpet for Christ to walk on. He made a red carpet for us to walk to the Father. His precious blood was spilled across the world. It was spilled abundantly. We too can spill our blood for love of him and our neighbor, drop by drop. It may not be as abundant as his was, but it will be a road sign for pilgrims to follow.

And so, contemplating sobornost in the poustinia, one must face being a pilgrim as the outcome. Once this contemplation in the poustinia is completed, once you have entered into the emptiness of God—the void* of God— you will see that things that are real belong to him, and all things that belong to you are as mist. You will see the mist is not worth turning your head to look at. Once this happens, somehow, by his immense grace, you will understand what it is that he is calling you to.

God the Father left a hunger in Adam and Eve, and God the Son brought an image of his face, for he said, "Who sees me sees the Father." Christ, the great Pilgrim who came from heaven down to earth and went from earth back to heaven, makes the dream of the pilgrim a reality.

There is no fogginess about that kind of thing. It is time to open the latch of your door, of the poustinia door, be it only the latch that is in your heart. (Many times I have repeated that you can have a poustinia of the heart and not go anyplace.) Be that as it may, now that you understand, now that you have passed through the void and know the void is never a void, you have met God. Now that you know he is there, you take your staff and go, leaving all things behind you.

You go to preach the gospel with your life—person to person—to anyone at any time. There is no rush. There is no rush at all. He who comes from the void of God is never rushed, for he bears within himself not only the image of God but the seal of his peace that surpasses all understanding.

So you go to the poustinia to contemplate unity, to

---

*When I mention "the void of God" I mean that state of prayer— beyond meditation and contemplation—when all senses are suspended and one rests in the peace of God and in his will.

bring forth mankind's dream that began with Adam and
Eve. The dream continues now because Christ was incarnate in our midst and has returned to heaven. Now we
know that we have to preach the gospel. A pilgrim preaches
the gospel, but in order to preach it he has to live it day by
day, hour by hour, minute by minute. For what is he
really about, that pilgrim of mine? He is preaching the
gospel with his life and so his pilgrimage has to reflect his
life.

It's a kind of strange pilgrimage. It's a new kind of
pilgrimage. It comes from the depths of a man. It was
there from time immemorial and it will be there until man
and God meet again in the parousia.

2. Following the Pilgrim Christ

Yes, it's a strange kind of pilgrimage, a new kind of pilgrimage, but it's also as old as man.

There is a way in which we can escape that pilgrimage. Oh, we can easily forget it! We can put a screen in our heart between it and all the rest of our life. We can go after many things. We can go on pilgrimages of our own —after gold, silver, fame, power, and so on. But those are not really pilgrimages. They are shams. They are imaginary goals that, once attained, fall apart and are replaced by other goals that become dust again. Ultimately, we remain empty.

True, everybody seems to be pilgrimaging. That is to say, human beings put one foot in front of the other all day long, resting a little at night. But one cannot apply the word "pilgrimage" to that sort of thing. That can be called a march. It can be called a "walking toward." It can be called by many names but it is not a pilgrimage. There are only two pilgrimages in life: one to heaven and one to hell.

Perhaps the one I am talking about here is a pilgrimage to hell, if hell is properly understood. It is a word much bandied about. But, like love, hell is totally indefinite. Our hell is first and foremost of our own making and our pilgrimage to it, because it is a pilgrimage, is also of our own making.

We want money. We want fame. We want this and we want that to satisfy our insatiable pleasure or need for pleasure or need for recognition or power. And it is to satisfy this selfish need that we create our own hell and we pilgrimage to it. It's a strange pilgrimage. It doesn't lead us anywhere except around and around and around. We can almost say that one meets oneself on such a pilgrimage and the circuit is very short and small. It is a small circle in which man walks because he obeys his will instead of God's! He has made it so. He worships his will. He follows it. And what happens? He worships emptiness. He follows emptiness and it leads him nowhere and because of that it is a hellish state to be in.

For a moment or two there is satisfaction. Satisfaction of having sensual pleasure, power, song, music—whatever you want to call it—but it vanishes long before the dawn comes, and as time goes on, even the dawns disappear. They merge with the night and man moves onward, following his own will in the dark.

One can't call that a pilgrimage except that the Prince of Evil leads it. Perhaps he relishes the word "pilgrimage" for his followers, but I wonder. I wonder.

Pilgrimage, the real one, the one I want to talk about, is holy. It started in the hearts of men when the doors of Eden were closed. Since then man has gone in search of the key. He knew there was going to be a key. He knew already the mercy of God then, for amusingly enough, if you want to call it amusing, in the bible the Lord provided a covering for Adam and Eve. He provided pelts or something like that, because it was going to be cold outside of paradise. It's a seldom noticed sentence but it is there; and man had hope.

This is one of the strange things about pilgrimages in search of God. Man has hope because he decides on a pilgrimage out of faith. When there is faith, there is always hope. When there is hope, there is love. Man is moved by hope, faith and love that somewhere, someplace, the key of paradise will be given to him again as Adam moves across the centuries. The pilgrimage was described in the bible and in other holy books which knew about the pilgrimage in search of the Absolute, in search of the key that would open the door to unity with the Absolute.

Many religions reflect that type of pilgrimage, and our own Christian faith reflects it very clearly. We were pilgrimaging in search of a key which we knew the mercy of God would hand us. In some cases his command was audible; in some cases hidden deep down in the hearts of men: "Arise and go. Go to seek me. Go to find me. Go to give me to others." That was the essence of the pilgrimage even in the Old Testament. Then Christ came and he was the key, the Key of David, that opened the door of paradise. Christ restored unity because he was the Key of David. He reunited the Trinity with man. Union with the Trinity was the goal of the heavenly pilgrimage that throughout the centuries men have undertaken.

The pilgrims couldn't do it alone. Even though their faith was like a fire, lighting the whole horizon; even though their hope was burning, shining against that faith like a match shines, leading toward the goal; even though love made the feet of the pilgrims indefatigable, constant and unfaltering, impervious to heat and cold (climates of the soul, I mean), still, man could not complete the journey without Christ.

Against the background of my thoughts, my understanding is dim and yet clear of the pilgrimage I speak about. But let us bring it down to every day, to the life of today. What role has pilgrimage in our technological world?

Again and again I pray over it. I pray over this thought which, like the root of a strange tree, has grown in my heart. Clear and unmistakable, so it seems to me, is this pilgrimage of man, the pilgrimage that must be if man and God are going to walk again together in the twilight, the sunny days, or early morning.

Again and again I come to the thought that, first, the pilgrim must pray, crying in the night like a child, sobbing like a woman. He must cry like men do, releasing unaccustomed tears out of eyes that haven't cried since childhood. That's what we must do. We must shed tears before the Almighty, asking for faith because we realize that nothing can happen in our relationship to God without faith.

So truly, out of the depths we cry to God. Out of the depths and heights of east and west we cry to God, but especially out of the night, the night brought by our technological society. The night in which machines continue to work 24 hours a day. There is no rest in the city from machines, from noise. There is no place to hide. We have to cry. In the middle of traffic, surrounded by huge trucks that make more noise than the trains of yore, we have to cry. We must cry to God to give us faith that we can be one again with him.

We don't believe it, you know. We really don't. We barely believe in the Pilgrim we call Jesus Christ. That's what I am talking about. We lack faith in the Trinity. The totality of love comes to us in the Trinity. "The Father so loved the Son that he gave his own Son." Listen to that! Listen! Look, look at that precipice on which he stood and from which he sent his Son to be crucified for you and me. Look at the cliff where love fell over the edge and gave his Son for you. Listen to the cries of the Son as he was flagellated, crucified. Here is a sea of pain the likes of which we cannot imagine unless we too are flagellated and crucified. And all for you and me!

In the resurrection, God handed you and me the key to the goal of our pilgrimage. We call it the doors of paradise, but there are many ways of explaining it. Still bloody from the wounds inflicted by his crucifixion, he hands you the key of reconciliation. It is the key of re-conciliation between God and man. That was the price of sobornost.

Now would you please meditate on sobornost? The meditation is so tremendous that we need to go apart, away, in solitude if possible, at least in the solitude of our hearts.

Christ the Reconciliator. Christ the Salvation of Man-kind. Christ the Victim. Christ Triumphant. Christ in our midst. Christ always present. Christ the Key to the Father.

This requires some thinking in a poustinia—the poustinia of the heart, the poustinia of a shack, the poustinia of a room—it makes no difference, but it requires meditation, deep and profound contemplation. This is the key. *Sobornost is the key to the survival of this planet,* believe it or not. *If we are united with God we will survive.* If we are not, we won't. So sobornost must be meditated upon, contemplated upon in the poustinia.

Why in the poustinia? Because the poustinia will strip away from us all that isn't God. Just think. Week after week, opening myself to God, to let him do with me as he wills, to concentrate on my oneness with him and my one-ness with my fellowmen. If I am one with God, I am one with men. Then and only then, when the poustinia has cleansed me totally, has opened me to God and to men, when my commitment is to the Lord God, to the Lord of History, to the Triune God, then leaving all things behind I move, because God has called me on a pilgrimage.

All people are called to pilgrimage, but not all answer,

and not all are called to the same pilgrimage. But the one I talk about is for those who are called to a pilgrimage that step by step follows the footsteps of Christ.

These pilgrims are easily seen because they leave bloody spots along the way. They are easily seen because there is a light coming from those spots. And now those pilgrims who are really pilgrims because God called them to be such pilgrims, having passed through meditating and contemplating sobornost and poustinia, are now making this rhythm—sobornost, poustinia and strannika (pilgrimage)—their way of life.

It is a strange pilgrimage. It is utterly unhurried. It is a pilgrimage whose only goal is the heart of God. It's not a pilgrimage to shrines. It's not a pilgrimage of seeing countries like so many young people have done lately. No. It's a pilgrimage that has one precious thing besides its poverty. It holds a key, and every day that key goes a little deeper into the heart of God until one day—*click!*—it will be open and man and God will be one. That kind of pilgrimage creates peace in order to give it to others, since man is in search of God and in search of peace from the raucous noise of the modern technological society.

It's a strange thing that the pilgrim who walks has the ability to stand still long enough to allow a neighbor to catch up with him.

It seems, therefore, that the pilgrimage of such people is formless. It is formless! Now he is here, helping somebody to build a house. Then when the house is built he moves on, walks long stretches, until God places before him another pitcher filled with the water of love and hope and of faith, and the towel of joy and consolation. And the pilgrim stops again. And again he performs that which is of need to someone else.

Maybe it will take him weeks. Maybe he appears to settle there wherever it is, but he never settles. He is always on the march. His particular task finished, he moves again. There is no settling down for such a pilgrim. Sometimes it may take him years to do what God asks of him, for example, create an apostolate, train such an apostolate, appear to be totally immersed in it for the stranger to see. But his heart is always waiting for the next call, for the Lord has for those people, the call of the mountain. Always the Lord says, "Come up higher. Friend, come higher!"

The pilgrim, being human, sometimes likes the spot where he has been placed. He wants to stay there. He wants to make a flower garden of that spot. Suddenly he hears, "Friend, come on higher!" and the pilgrim turns his face and sees the mountain of the Lord. There is snow up there. He can hear the cold wind and he clutches the key that was given to him by the resurrected Christ to go higher, to enter a little deeper into God's heart, to enter a little more into sobornost, to do his will better, faster, more joyfully as a voyager. It's not easy, for the voice keeps repeating, "Friend, come on higher!"

3. From Refugee to Pilgrim

YES, GOD ALWAYS SEEMS to call a soul to "come higher." I have often wondered: what kind of mountain does he call us to? They tell me that Mount Sinai is the mountain of the Lord, and so it is, for many things happened on it. But I don't think that is the kind of mountain that he is calling people to climb. Rather he calls us to a very special mountain. A mountain that grows according to his words.

I speculate on all this because I am a pilgrim. This statement needs qualification, for I think I am right when I believe that God has guided me in some way to be a pilgrim.

Well, let us consider a little bit of my life. I must do so in order to pass on the idea of pilgrimage to others.

I was born in Russia. I received no special revelation that I was going to be a pilgrim. Nothing even remotely resembling such a calling came to me. I was firmly planted in the soil of Russia and the soil of Russia was firmly planted in me—in my heart too. As I grew up I visualized marriage, children, farm life in the country (for I come from farming stock). But all this suffered a tremendous blow, first, with World War I and, second, with the Communist revolution. You might say that in the twinkling of an eye I was transplanted, thrown out, separated, torn away from my homeland. I became a "refugee." To be planted in your own country, to know that your family has been there 800 years, or more maybe, and then suddenly to become a refugee, well, this was almost unthinkable. It was to me.

And when my husband and I crossed the border of Finland (which appeared to be a little more peaceful than Russia), Finland didn't prove to be very friendly. Eventually we escaped from Finland and finally came to England, onto what you might call "free soil." There I sat down one day on the very top of a large building, the YMCA of Edinburgh. The YMCA had very generously given us a room, for Boris, my husband, had pleurisy and was just out of the hospital. Anyhow, I sat on a chair on the very top of that YMCA building. Boris was sleeping. I suddenly got hit with the word "refugee." It seemed that the first time I took a breath in a free country, I realized I was a refugee.

Do you know what saved my sanity at that time? I thought of Jesus Christ, of Mary and of Joseph. They were refugees. An angel told Joseph to take Jesus and his Mother to Egypt. I said to myself, "Why do you use the word 'refugee'? Why don't you use the word 'pilgrim'?" It was at that moment when I realized that Jesus Christ had been a refugee too. He was a pilgrim even at that early age in the natural order of things. Somehow I felt comforted.

In that upstairs room in the city of Edinburgh I found the root idea of pilgrimage: *God pilgrimaged, why shouldn't I?* He fled from his enemies, why shouldn't I? God blessed the land of Egypt by his presence, why shouldn't I follow in his footsteps and be blessed by his resurrected presence in any land at any time? I felt comforted.

But it's time for me to begin to tell you the preparations that I now see God made for me to become a pilgrim. For God prepares us for those things.

I look back on my childhood and youth and the first thing I see is that my mother was a pilgrim. She went to visit monasteries, convents and holy places. She would go to see an icon that was renowned for its miracles and its "compassion," as mother used to say. Well, the preparations for those pilgrimages were very simple. My mother would say to me a week or a few days before she planned to go to this place or that place that I should make ready to do likewise. She meant that I should see to it that my rough linen shift was in good shape and clean, that the *lapti* (birchbark shoes) were soft and fitted my feet. (Usually, before a pilgrimage, you had to ask a skilled man to fit you with birchbark shoes.) Then, you also had to get a bag made out of linen. It crisscrossed your shoulders from left to right, very much like water bags. In it would be a loaf of black bread and a little bit of salt. On the other shoulder, crisscrossing from right to left, would be a gourd of water. Then there would be an icon on a cord hanging in front. Also there was something for your head. The men wore hats of some sort; the women kerchiefs, also made of linen.

I can't remember wearing anything else, for when it rained I remember being wet and mother saying, "Walking dries the rain out." But usually we could go and hide from the rain in a barn someplace. Those were my first recollections to true pilgrimages where we put one foot in front of the other. Most of the time we went barefoot. *Laptis* were for rain.

I remember something else. I remember that sometime around the age of 11 or 12 I decided to become a "holy pilgrim" myself—without my mother! I too could go and pray in some convent, monastery or such. So I put on the garb of a pilgrim, though it was autumn, and in the fall you could of course change your garb. You could wear a black skirt, a black blouse and a heavy sweater, and a cape if the weather was inclement. And always the icon on your breast. Your head was covered with a black kerchief, sort of nunnish-looking. Anyhow, that's how I dressed myself and proceeded to go on a pilgrimage.

I made my way down the main avenue of Petrograd (now Leningrad), crossing innumerable bridges. Petrograd has many bridges because it is built on islands. I finally got to the big highway outside the city. As I was walking up that highway and wondering whether I should knock on somebody's door and ask for shelter for the night, a two-horse-drawn vehicle stopped and a policeman came out and said, "Are you Miss So-and-So?" I said, "Yes." "Well," he said, "your father would like you to come home." So I climbed in the vehicle and they brought me home.

My father merely said: "Catherine, you always wanted to be a pilgrim, but how can you be a pilgrim without the blessing of your parents? You just walked away without saying anything, and certainly without a blessing." That was all he said. I felt sorely ashamed and miserable. Of course you couldn't walk out of your parents' home without a blessing. (Actually you should have the blessing of the parish priest also.) But I had walked out by myself, slightly arrogant. So I had been a pilgrim before I was really even a teenager. The idea of pilgrimage had already taken shape in my heart.

Years later, as refugees, we left Scotland for England, and England for Canada. When I came to Canada I felt like a pilgrim indeed, although I had not chosen this particular pilgrimage. Secondly, I was a stranger in a strange land, but a pilgrim is never a stranger to any land because he lives in the resurrected Christ and all the earth is his. Somehow or other it *was* a pilgrimage, but the word "refugee" was more suited to me at the moment. I think that's the way God planned it. You have to cut out some roots to put others in.

All Christians must make a pilgrimage. They must make a journey inward to meet the God that dwells within them. May I share with you this poem I once wrote about pilgrimage?

JOURNEY INWARD

My soul hungered
For God
Before it was clothed
With flesh.

But when it became
Imprisoned
In the flesh that is
It fell asleep.

And those who sleep
Know hunger not.

Somewhere along
The road of life
By the grace of
God,
My soul woke up

And its hunger
Now,
Became a fire.

A fire that consumed
Me.
Ate me up
With its intense
Devouring heat.

I could not rest
Anywhere
Except in motion,

In a motion that
Led me to
God.

That is how I
Began
The journey inward.

That long, endless
Journey
That every soul
Must undertake

If she is to meet
Her God.

It is a strange
Journey,
Across arid plains,
And verdant valleys,
Dried parchment-like
Deserts.

A journey of many
Crossroads
And endless
Sharp turns.

That confuse
And clamor
For a rest.

But the hunger
For God,
Knows no rest.
So I go on,
And on, and on.

Yes, it is a strange
Journey,
That slowly
Makes me shed
All the baggage
I took for it

The baggage I took
For it,
Before I knew
That it was
Too heavy a load
For this kind of
Journey.

I don't know where
I left it
Somewhere
Back there
By some crossroad.

Now I am baggage-less
But somehow
Still too heavily
Burdened,

My hunger drives me
On.
But now for speedy
Traveling it
Demands,

I must start
Shedding my
Clothing.

There, on this stone
I must lay
The cloak
Of selfishness
That kept me warm.

It is cold
Without it,
But I can walk
Faster,
As my hunger
Urges me
To.

Here, on this branch
I must hang
My dress of
Self-love
And compromise
With the world.

I shiver now,
In earnest
But my feet
Seem to have
Wings.

Yet this sheltered
Rock
Begs for my
Underwear.

Slowly, reluctantly
I shed one by one
My undergarments—
Here goes self-
Indulgence.

Tidily, next to it,
I lay greed for
Possessions, and
Love of ease and
Comfort.

Next, not so
Tidily go
Helter-skelter
All the things
In me that are
Not God's.

Lord, behold
I stand naked
Before Thee,
With wings on
My feet.

With wings on
My feet.
Now my journey
Inward
Will be swift.

But it is
Not.
For I still
Stumble
And fall, and
Walk haltingly
Inches, instead of
Miles.

While the hunger for
God
Flays me and
Urges me to make
Haste.

Oh, I had forgotten
The shoes—
The heavy, comfortable
Shoes
That have shielded
My feet.

Shielded my feet
From the cutting
Stones.
From the sharp
Pebbles.

I must unlace
My shoes.
My comfortable
Stout shoes.

The last covering
Of my naked body.
The last stronghold
Of my non-surrender
To God.

I hesitate.
The narrow path
Upwards
Is so hard.

It has so many
So many sharp
Stones.

So many knife-edged
Pebbles.

But the hunger
For God
Flames in me
A furnace of fire
Unquenchable.

The fire of love
Of passionate
Utter love
Of God.

I must go on
On that journey
Inward
That alone
Will bring me
Face to face

With him
For whom I hunger
Constantly
Without ceasing.

Quickly I bend
With hasty clumsy
Fingers
I unlace one
Shoe
Then the other.

My eagerness
Is becoming part
Of my hunger

Recklessly
I throw
One shoe—this way
The other—that.

Not caring
Whither which falls
And now
I am free.

I am free
And naked
And my feet
Have huge wings

Huge wings
That carry me
Across the sharp
Stones

And the knife-edged
Pebbles
Without harm

Now brambles and
Thorns that edge
The path
Open up
And point
The other way.

I am a naked
Soul
Free and untrammeled
Driven by the
Hunger of my love
For God.

Driven by my love for
God . . . on and on . . .
On this journey
Inward.

I did not know
It was going to
Be so easy
Now that I
Shed all my
Garments.

But now I KNOW
For my hunger is
Being assuaged
Satiated—filled
Even
As I fly
On my winged feet.

Along the steep
Path upward.
It is being filled
That hunger of mine
So much, so well

That I can feed
Others
With the surplus
Of the food given to me
So abundantly.

Yes, my soul hungered
For God,
Before it was even
Clothed with flesh

God meets
The soul
That starts
On its journey inward
Half way.

Provided the soul
Driven by its
Hunger of love
For him
Strips itself
Naked.

That is the secret
Of his love
And of his kingdom
That begins
Even on this earth.

But the price
I repeat
Is nakedness
Complete.
Even unto
Discarding
Shoes . . .

4. "The Soles of My Feet Were Bloody"

THE POEM IN THE PREVIOUS CHAPTER presents the pilgrimage of the soul toward the God that dwells within it. And so, of course, I entered into that pilgrimage. But I also entered into the pilgrimage of service. It seems as though God was shaping me "to serve." I was a waitress, a laundress, a sales clerk, a nurse, a maid in a private house, all jobs that entailed walking. Always walking. And I realized at the time—and that consoled me much—that all this walking was fulfilling God's desire or injunction, "I have come to serve." If he had come to serve, so had I, so waiting and being a maid and being a laundress meant service.

Pilgrims in Russia pray all the time. There is silence and prayer, psalms and song. The songs, of course, are holy ones. You walk together barefooted, you pray together, you sing together, and you are silent together. So I sang this journey inward side-by-side with the journey of service outward and I was seemingly fulfilling what God said, "Pray always," which is always a preparation for a pilgrimage. I had to pray always because the pilgrimage of pain was with me, deep and profound.

There was the loss of my husband, Boris, first through the annulment of our marriage, then through death, but especially, at that time, through the annulment. There was loneliness, the feeling more than ever of being a stranger in a strange land. Being a Polak didn't help in a land which, in those days, kowtowed to the rich and the WASPS. All this created an atmosphere of true pilgrimage, the true pilgrimage inward that every man must make to meet his God. The pilgrimage of pain is the pilgrimage of prayer, and the pilgrimage of service.

Yes, it was in this school that I began to really understand what pilgrimage was. Eventually I got a position which paid $20,000 a year. It didn't require walking as before, and I got over the pain a little, and things quieted down. But a new idea came. Though the pilgrimage of pain subsided, I was still walking the journey inward, for you walk the journey inward all your life to meet the God who dwells within. My pilgrimage of service changed because of a change of jobs and positions.

First I was lecturing, and then I became an executive in a lecture bureau, work which took me across America and Europe. As I lectured, a strange thought kept coming. I usually had a bible—a little one for travel and a big one at home—and whenever I opened that bible, or any other bible, for some reason it always opened to the words: "If any man would come after me, let him deny himself and take up his cross daily and follow me."

Well, I used to meditate on that and periodically I wrote down on little pieces of paper, envelopes and such, thoughts that came from the bible, or just my own mind. As I traveled, I would drop them in my purse. One day I got to thinking, "Why is it that I always open bibles at the same passage?" "Well," I said to myself, "they are worn and torn so they automatically open at that passage."

I went to a friend. She had a bible. I opened it. It was new, but behold, there was the passage! I got a little frightened and I said, "I'll go to the library in New York." They have beautiful illustrated bibles about two feet wide, hard to handle but beautiful. I closed my eyes again and opened it. I turned the pages, and *boom!* The same passage! Well, it made a girl think! I returned home. I gathered up all the little writings I had jotted down. Lying flat on the floor, I gathered them all together in some sort of order, and they came out just like this:

Arise—go! Sell all you possess . . . give it directly, personally to the poor. Take up My cross (their cross) and follow Me—going to the poor—being poor—being one with them—one with Me.

Little—be always little . . . simple—poor—child-like.

Preach the gospel *with your life—without compromise*—listen to the Spirit—he will lead you.

Do little things exceedingly well for love of Me.

Love—love—love, never counting the cost.

Go into the marketplace and stay with Me . . . pray . . . fast . . . pray always . . . fast.

Be hidden—be a light to your neighbor's feet. Go without fears into the depths of men's hearts . . . I shall be with you.

Pray always. *I will be your rest.*

I typed it out myself. I looked at it and said to myself, *"This is biblical!"* I had a fear, a tremendous fear in my heart, because I felt as if God's hand was in it. When I say "fear" I mean "awe." It was rather clear what I should do. I started a pilgrimage to priests. My son was still small, though well taken care of in many ways. The priests were unable to give me any advice.

I wanted to sell all I possessed and go on a real pilgrimage, a lifelong pilgrimage, a pilgrimage on which there is no real earthly home. Everybody is a home who needs me.

So I remembered what my mother and father said: "Whenever you are in a real difficulty spiritually, go to the father of your soul who is the Ordinary of the diocese, be it a bishop, Archbishop or Cardinal. Go to him and ask. He has the fullness of the gifts of God." So I went to see Archbishop Neil MacNeil of Toronto. He listened very carefully and did not doubt my desire but said to wait a while, which is what I did.

Sometime afterwards the Archbishop agreed, so I literally sold all I possessed. With a small suitcase I went down to Portland Street in the slums of Toronto where I rented a room in a humble place. My idea was to pray and serve the people. They were all, at that time, Polish, Russian, Ukrainian—very poor people. It was depression time. So the first part of the "Mandate" as I call it now—the Little Mandate—became a reality; namely, I had sold all I possessed, I had taken up my cross and I had followed him.

It appeared to be just exactly what I wanted and what I felt sure God wanted, for he was sending me on a pilgrimage that would grow. I felt that I would someday leave that room, start walking, perhaps hitchhike—for this is a different part of the world than Russia—and stop at places where I was needed. I would travel without money, just as pilgrims should do.

It is good to read *The Story of the Other Wise Man* by Henry Van Dyke to understand the situation of the pilgrim. In the story three Wise Men undertook a tremendous pilgrimage to see a Child in a manger. The fourth man didn't make it, so the legend says, because he kept serving while pilgrimaging. That's what I thought pilgrimage would be for me too.

But God directs you quite differently than your own thoughts. This is why you always have to fold the wings of your intellect and open the door of your heart. This is why you always have to listen, and listen well, to the voice of God, for in the twinkling of an eye he may bid the pilgrim to stand still.

Then the pilgrimage of movement, of traveling in the resurrected Christ, is somehow or other encompassed in a strange stillness, in learning to listen, learning how to be still. However, the Lord obviously meant that though I would still be a pilgrim, as I will explain later, I would not be alone. There came three women and two men who desired to join me, and the Bishop suggested I take them. This I did.

Thus was begun Friendship House and what is today Madonna House.

I must admit that it took me quite a while to recover, for I had so beautifully arranged everything—my prayer life, my serving life. Suddenly, God mixed it all up. He said, "Friend, come up higher." I thought he would have said, "Come on lower," but he didn't. He said, "Come up higher."

I must admit that at that time this sentence didn't sit too well with me. Poverty, the poor around me, the prospect of further pilgrimages, all this surrounded me like a green valley. I had no wish to climb any mountain of the Lord. I could feel the cold of the place to which he was calling me and the snowflakes were already melting on my face. I didn't want to go up. I preferred to go down but he said in his inimitable fashion, "Friend, come up higher."

And so I went into a turbulence of snow and ice and cold winds. It took me a long time to realize that even then I was on a pilgrimage.

Always, always, my heart pilgrimaged, and so did I, crisscrossing the continents of Europe and America. I lectured. Well, that's a nice way of saying that I preached in season and out of season the gospel of the Lord.

First and foremost in the early 30's I preached on behalf of the silent ones, those who had no jobs, those who were crying out for social justice; later on, the issue was interracial justice.

The pilgrimage was hard. I wanted desperately to be alone. I wanted the poustinia. I wanted a reunion with God that would make me feel united with men. I was united with them but they somehow were not united with me in social justice or in interracial justice. Rotten eggs and tomatoes were thrown at me. But the pilgrimage continued. It was a difficult one.

As I said, I crisscrossed the continents. Six times I crossed the U.S.A., for one reason or another. Three or four times Canada, from Halifax and Sydney to British Columbia.

I was not a very welcome pilgrim. Oh yes, they made arrangements for my coming. They paid me the money they said they would, but I was unpopular. Sometimes pilgrims have to be unpopular. In *The Way of a Pilgrim* it is related that one time the Pilgrim was preaching the gospel in his own fashion and somebody got angry with him and took him to the police. He was beaten and put in jail for 24 hours. He was holy, and he rejoiced at that.

Well, I wasn't a Russian pilgrim in that sense. I just kept one foot in front of the other because I knew I had to pilgrimage. I had to pilgrimage to preach the gospel to people who didn't really want to hear it. That was a strange pilgrimage.

God again said, "Come on higher," and I thought I

was going to an even colder place than before. But it wasn't. It turned out to be a desert. In this desert there were strange figures that kept stoning me for some reason or other. But I survived.

It was a strange pilgrimage. I thought of my mother and her bare feet and, in a manner of speaking, I imagined walking deserts with bare feet, the deserts of Tennessee, of Alabama, of Kentucky, of Florida and of other southern states.

I traveled. I spoke. I did what pilgrims have to do. A pilgrim is always preaching the word of God. Preach the gospel with your life, not necessarily with your mouth. But I spoke it then. There are no words to describe the weariness I experienced. Preaching interracial justice in the South in those days was a wearisome thing. I don't blame them for their opposition. They were victims of their social conditioning.

Cold and deserts. I lived in them quite a long time. Yes, for a long time. Yet, it was a true pilgrimage just the same because it was directed by God, and I walked toward the goals that God meant me to have. My pilgrimage brought charity, social justice—in a word, it brought the gospel to a lot of people. Whether they accepted it or not I wouldn't know. All I know is that "the soles of my feet were bloody." All the time I walked on pavements. I had lovely rooms, beautiful convents, lovely monasteries and hotels, but somehow or other the soles of my feet were bloody. That, my friends, is also part of a pilgrimage.

5. Pilgrimage to the Hearts of Men

YES, MY FEET WERE BLOODY because, quite evidently, I was still pilgrimaging. I was on a pilgrimage that was both outward, and, as I wrote in my poem, inward. I had unlaced my shoes. I had thrown away everything that was not God's, as the poem says, my undergarments and my cloak of selfishness and all the rest. So I thought, anyhow. But I knew for sure that all this lecturing and all this standing still in Friendship House and in Madonna House was a pilgrimage.

The strangest thing was that, when I read and reread the Little Mandate, it kept jumping around in my mind, and I suddenly knew why my feet were bloody: I was going into the depths of men's hearts. That is a precipitous pilgrimage. The depths are stony and they wound your feet. You walk on sharp gravel. You try to hold on to something but there is nothing to hold on to. So, when you go into the depths of men's hearts, your feet get bloody.

I said to myself, Why? It took me quite a while to find out why. Going into men's hearts is a precipitous descent because men's hearts are deep; it is taking the pain of men upon yourself. I suddenly realized that there was something much deeper and more profound in pilgrimage than just bloody feet. It was the carrying of another man's cross. Crosses have a way of biting into your shoulders and into your back. That's when I realized that I was still on pilgrimage even though it wasn't the way I had thought about it. It was the way God had thought about it. And in a sort of strange bouncing manner, like a ball, I was fulfilling the Little Mandate as God wished me to.

Of course, I had given away everything as he had asked me. The whole Mandate was there in my heart, as far as I was concerned. I had given everything up; I had gone to the poor; I had lived in the marketplace; I was poor with him and poor with them and I hoped that all the things that the Mandate said were at least germinating in me even though they hadn't attained full flowering. It takes a long while to attain such flowering. But I had begun.

The Mandate said, "Go into the depths of men's hearts—I shall be with you." Well, that is another pilgrimage and an important one. It doesn't apply only to me. It applies to everyone. It applies to all Christians and perhaps it applies even to non-Christians, for the Lord is the Lord of History.

Why did this strange idea come to me, this pilgrimage into men's hearts, and its application to everyone, especially to all Christians? Because such a pilgrimage can be undertaken only with love and not with any ordinary human love. Human love doesn't want precipitous descents into men's hearts. It doesn't want to have bloody feet. It doesn't want to have bloody backs and deep scars from other people's crosses. Men don't want that, but God does, and men in love with God can't help themselves. They have to embark on this pilgrimage because God has given us fantastic gifts that we do not understand completely.

For instance, we have the gift of assisting Christ in his saving work, strange as this might seem. We can assist him because he invited us to do so. "It makes me happy to suffer for you, as I am suffering now, and in my own body to do what I can to make up all that has still to be undergone by Christ for the sake of his body, the Church" (Col 1:24). We have also the gift of miracles, for Christ said, "I tell you most solemnly, whoever believes in me will perform the same works as I do myself; he will perform even greater works because I am going to the Father" (Jn 14:12).

So I stood before that strange revelation in my heart. It was as if something were made clear to me. It was as if the Holy Spirit had shed his light on me. He flashes his light suddenly, on one word, on one sentence of the gospel or the scriptures, and what was unfamiliar yesterday becomes familiar today. It becomes a whole new gift of God. We often take this word for granted, but there is nothing in the gospel that can be taken for granted.

So this clarity came to me, and I understood a little better what pilgrimage was.

Yes, it was a pilgrimage that one had to undertake, everyone had to undertake, every Christian, to meet the God who dwells within. It was a pilgrimage that went outwards, barefooted, to worship the face of Christ someplace —to pray in a monastery that was holy, or to go to a shrine that was renowned. These were pilgrimages, but there was so much more to it.

There is, of course, the pilgrimage of life that people love to discuss. "Life is a pilgrimage!" is found in so many novels, but who probes the depths of that pilgrimage? Who knows its pains and its joys? Very few. Very, very few. I understand that we should be quite simple, and I mean simple in the simplest way—childlike—about miracles. If we have faith we can encircle with our love anyone whom we meet on the road who is in need of a miracle; and we in the same faith can perform that miracle. We can say, "Thy faith and the blessing of Jesus Christ have made thee whole." We can say that because, as any pilgrim of Christ knows very well, without God he is nothing and he can never attribute to himself anything at all. All that he does he does through God. Somehow or other the pilgrim becomes a road through which the fire of God travels and tries to ignite a responsive fire in men.

Yes, I thought much about pilgrimages. Deep down in my heart—call it a dream—the desire of pilgrimage persists even now; the desire to be of service and to pray somewhere else than where I am. At the moment, nothing can happen to me, and nothing will happen to me, but to those who read this book it might be that they have heard in the night the voice of Christ saying, "Arise. Take up your cross and follow me." They may become actual pilgrims. But that's up to God, and up to the heart that is open to him.

I realize many things as I grow older. I realize that the pilgrim is one who also stands still. It's not easy to stand still. It requires a tremendous amount of patience, and it requires a tremendous faith in God that is almost unshakeable. Hence it requires constant prayer: "Lord, I believe. Help my unbelief!"

Yes, a pilgrimage is also standing still. It is not just standing still. Stillness is beautiful. Silence is delectable. All true, but that's not what I am talking about. I am talking about a strange form of pilgrimage. It's so hard to explain it. It's so hard to explain what happens between a human heart and God, because he who said, "Arise—come, take up your cross and follow me" suddenly turns around and says, "Stand still—completely still—as I stood before the Sanhedrin, before Pilate, before the Roman soldiers and even through my flagellation. There will come a day when you will learn the goal of the pilgrimage that I ask you to undertake." You will stand in perfect stillness because your hands and feet are nailed. You are unable to walk. That's a pilgrimage too. In fact, it is a supreme pilgrimage. In a way, a crown of pilgrimages.

Right now there is this request of God to stand still.
Not for silence alone. Not for solitude. Not for any of
these things. But to stand in the middle of a road for
people to come to the pilgrim. Oh, they will know he is a
pilgrim. His hands are empty. His feet are bare, in a
manner of speaking. He has a little roll on his back which
is like a cape that he will sleep on. He carries a linen bag
filled with bread, salt and water. All this is not seen by
men's eyes, but it is there. It has to be envisaged, for he
lives by the Eucharist and he drinks of the living waters of
Christ.

How does one know he is a pilgrim? His face reflects
the Pilgrim-Icon of Christ. He stands still and lets others
come to him and he answers their questions. This is hard,
this strange standing still that God demands of pilgrims at
one time or another! Now questions are shouted at the
pilgrim, whispered at the pilgrim, spoken to the pilgrim!
It's astonishing that the pilgrim doesn't die or doesn't go
insane under this barrage of questions. None of this happens because he is in love with God! And since the questions are all about God (for nobody asks a question of a
pilgrim that does not deal with God), he gets the grace to
answer them.

Yes, it's a strange pause in a pilgrimage, this request
of God to stop and to allow others to come. It is another
form of preaching the gospel without compromise.

The pilgrim is wide open. People can look behind
him, in front of him, at his side. There is little to see.
There is the crust of bread and the gourd of water. That's
all. So people begin to believe that maybe he can answer
their questions. Above all, they begin to experience they
are not as lonely as they were before. Though pilgrims are
lonely people, walking alone most of the time, they can
create an atmosphere among people of joy, of friendship,

and of understanding. The pilgrim doesn't do it, but he has discovered how to allow God to do it all.

So pilgrimage embraces also that strange pause which God seems to demand of all pilgrims. The pause of total stillness and of being available to anyone. (I translate this, for as I said, it is hard to explain things that exist between God and man, myself and God. I try to explain it simply.)

Pilgrimage is also symbolic. It's not a question of standing on a road and blocking the traffic or something like that. Not at all. It is fulfilling the Little Mandate, living in the marketplace, for the marketplace is a place where men gather. So this stillness exists, takes place in the marketplace. There again the pilgrim touches the depths of men's hearts.

As one listens to all those screaming, whispering cries of despair, to those cries of hope that men bring to a pilgrim, one becomes cognizant again why his feet are bloody. Because he who enters the hearts of men enters a new world. One cannot describe it geographically. One can describe it as an immense, new—totally new—land: the land of God. The land where sometimes the battle of Jesus Christ and the devil in the desert is repeated.

So when you enter the hearts of men, you might possibly be entering at the moment when the devil is tempting man in the same way that he tempted Jesus Christ. So vast is the land of souls, so immense is the land of hearts, that a pilgrim enters in the spirit of the gospel. No wonder the feet of the pilgrim are bloody, for the hearts of men are often stony—fragmented stones, not easy to walk upon.

Strange! Pilgrims must be also totally defenseless and absolutely open. There must be about them a very child-like simplicity. A pilgrim cannot pilgrimage if he hides anything in his heart. He must be open. Totally open, to anyone.

I remember the days when everything I did and said was questioned. I was, in fact, a *persona non grata* for many, many years of our 47-year-old apostolate. It's only since Vatican II that some modicum of popularity has come to Madonna House. But I am not talking about Madonna House. I am talking about pilgrimage.

The pilgrim is totally open. He is not afraid of persecution. He accepts persecution because he is the follower of a persecuted God. A pilgrim is a person of pain. If he is not ready to accept pain he cannot be a pilgrim. Pain walks with him night and day. But strangely enough, joy does too.

Yes, there is a secret about pilgrimages: the acceptance of pain. The very sentences, "Arise and go," "Take up my cross and follow me," spell pain. "Arise. Leave everything that is around and about you that is familiar and go, not knowing where or why. Take up my cross and follow me." The mere thought of taking up Christ's cross and following him somewhere . . . nowhere . . . no place . . . is frightening, and when that fear gets hold of you your pilgrimage ceases.

Fear is conquered by faith. Because your heart is faith-full, and because you love the God who calls you into the nowhere, contrary to every half-inch of your intellect, contrary to everything, you go! When you stand in front of the cross that he has allotted you, it is always heavy. But he is generous. His cross grows or shrinks depending on the person he has called. Looking at his cross, the would-be pilgrim wants to run away, but he can't, he just can't, because love holds him tight. So he bends down and he puts that cross on his shoulders and he goes, not knowing where, because he trusts, like Abraham when God asked him to sacrifice his son.

Yes, we have to show the faithful the way, so we go,

those of us who are called to the pilgrimage. We go, filled with a burning pain that seems to eat our very entrails, a pain so annihilating that when we look at ourselves we seem to be a shadow walking. My shadow . . . the pilgrim. And yet, suddenly, joy floods the soul. The pilgrim stands straight and carries the cross for others as if it were a feather, because he has heard the song of the Trinity, because he dances to its tune with little steps, walking onward to the nowhere to which God calls him. Pain and joy intermingle in pilgrimages.

Remember that pilgrims pray all the time. Having passed from the prayer of petition, to the prayer of meditation, to the prayer of contemplation, it is possible that the pilgrim might enter into the void of God where all senses are suspended. Then, of course, he doesn't feel the cross, although it is still there. He now is united to the Most Holy Trinity. And now and again it seems to him as he walks on that he can hear the footsteps of God at eventide.

Now the sense of pilgrimage becomes clear. If his prayer has not yet brought him to this void where all senses are suspended, it has brought him to contemplation of him whom he loves. Love will urge the pilgrim on no matter what. Because love is like that. The reason why he started on that pilgrimage is because his Lover told him to do so.

You see, he has been schooled in the school of sobornost. Remember? He has spent much time in the poustinia, to meditate and understand the sobornost that must exist between God and man his brother. And then God has come to him and said, "Arise and come. Take up my cross and follow me," and he has done so. He started with sobornost. So, even while he is in the state of meditation and contemplation, his faith hears the footsteps of God in the cool of the evening, and the ancient remembrance, the ancient dream becomes a reality.

6. Leaving the Poustinia

YES, THE PILGRIM HEARS, besides his own footsteps (even when he stands still), the footsteps of God as he passes by at eventide, even as Adam and Eve heard him.

Yes, again, a pilgrimage is a strange thing. To go on a pilgrimage in the old days was virtuous. You gave alms to the poor and you pilgrimaged to the holy places. That was a simplification—a beautiful one—of the pilgrimage.

But pilgrimage is so much more, so terribly much more, and so hard to explain. For myself even, I have to constantly go over the rosary of pilgrimage. It is all that the old-timers said: an act of devotion. But it's more. It requires sobornost to begin, and it requires the poustinia to internalize sobornost, for it really to take hold—to reunite yourself to God and man—which is what sobornost means. It requires the silence and solitude of a poustinia for this to happen, be it a real poustinia or the poustinia of your heart. It doesn't matter very much, but it must be an entry into one's own depths, depths that lie unsuspected in the hearts of all men.

Poustinia, sobornost, union, and a steeping of oneself in that union. One has to steep oneself. Factually, one has to become totally immersed in that union, for sobornost is a unity that must not be broken.

So the grains of that funny rosary fall from my hands, one by one. So far there might have been one or two or maybe three familiar grains, but now I come to a strange one. A rather large one. It is the experience of the poustinik, who has immersed himself in sobornost as far as he can or could, and who arises from his chair or bed and moves toward the door of his poustinia. If he has the solitude of the heart, he moves to the door of his heart because now, faintly yet clearly, he hears the voice of God saying, "Arise and come into the marketplace and preach the Good News to all you meet."

The poustinik is unsure for a moment or two. He has spent so long, it seems to him, absorbing or being absorbed in sobornost—the unity that God meant from the beginning to exist between man and God and man and his brother. It took such a long time for that immersion, and all of it was spent in the poustinia, for sobornost needs silence and solitude and a deep listening heart.

Now suddenly, quite unexpectedly, God calls and says, "Come. Arise and come into the marketplace and preach the Good News." No wonder the pilgrim hesitates. He knew that he would be called to a pilgrimage but he did not know what kind of pilgrimage. And the pilgrimage of the marketplace was the furthest from his thoughts. He visualized a lonely road . . . city pavements and city streets, yes, but he pictured himself passing by, as it were, bearing the icon of Christ on his face and his heart, leaving the city, going into country places, onto rural roads, little paths, little roads, to little people, not crowds. Yet he hears the voice: "Arise. Come into the marketplace and preach my gospel with your life."

It is no wonder that the pilgrim hesitates, for he is somewhat new to this accent of pilgrimages. He really enters into the land of faith. He does not know where it leads or how he is going to walk it. Will it be hard or easy? What is meant by preaching the gospel with his life?

All this is not quite a jumble in the mind of the pilgrim, but it is something that he has to pray about. Again he has to make a leap into faith. A new one. Always, "Come up higher." The words of Christ, "Come up higher," really do not mean a mountain like Mount Sinai, but the mountain of faith. It is so difficult these days to have faith.

The beginning of the pilgrimage is another leap into a new aspect of faith. No wonder the would-be pilgrim stops at the door of his heart or hut to ponder, for the marketplace is a threatening place. Nevertheless, the voice of the Lord in his heart is clear, "Come out and preach the gospel with your life."

It reminds me of a little story told about Catherine of Siena who was a contemplative and a mystic. She used to live in the basement of her house because her mother didn't like her being so religious; so she allotted her that spot. She spent her time praying to God and being close to him and he was with her in that basement cell. One day he said to her, "Come. Arise and go" (into what amounted to the marketplace of that day) "and nurse and help the people." She wouldn't do it. She was very comfortable with him in the basement. He said to her, "If you don't go, I won't be here."

Well, that's just a legend maybe. I don't know. But the point remains that the pilgrim understands that he has to go, because if he doesn't go God will turn his face away from him, in a manner of speaking. Or, to put it another way, the pilgrim will sadden the heart of God.

So he goes. He is so new at it. He doesn't know how to preach the gospel with his life. He just keeps being poor, chaste and obedient. He may take a menial job of some sort for a while, but wherever he goes something happens. People change. At first he doesn't understand that now he is pilgrimaging not in the marketplace but in the hearts of people. He has gone down to the hearts of men, as God bade him to do, for the only way to preach anything is to be silent and carry the cross of man.

Now he begins to understand his role in the marketplace, or wherever he goes, whether on the small little grass roads or the pavement of the cities. He has to enter the hearts of men, and the only way to enter, the only key that allows men to enter the hearts of others is *identifying* oneself with the other. This identification is excruciating. It takes faith to identify oneself with another.

Well, the pilgrim masters this slowly and God is his teacher. The pilgrim is like a novice. I repeat again, he is like a novice. He has to be taught. But once he masters it there comes a time when he pauses in his pilgrimage of the marketplace and of all kinds of places, because again he hears the voice, "Stand still. Take off your shoes. The place is holy." He takes off his shoes, figuratively speaking, and prepares himself for the next step in his pilgrimage.

The next step doesn't happen to many. It happens to a few, for the Lord is merciful. But those who have taken off their shoes and have realized that the place is holy now understand the width, the depth and the height of what is meant by "preaching the gospel with your life." Now it's not a marketplace of unbelievers who do not care, of believers who are very weak, of true believers, of pagans. Now the pilgrim faces a very simple thing, for God speaks to him of a *total identification with himself.* Not only with his brethren; this is past. This is there already. But gently, yet forcefully, he calls the pilgrim to come to his supper, to partake of his bread and of his wine, and to follow him to Gethsemani, along the way of the cross, right unto Golgotha. He presents him with the sight of a cross on which he will have to lie and on which he will have to be crucified. It is not anymore the carrying of somebody's cross that breaks the skin of your shoulder. It is not even experiencing Pontius Pilate's Roman soldiers with their whips. It is none of those things.

Now the pilgrim knows. Now everything is clear. This was the reason why he had to be immersed in sobornost in the poustinia. This is the reason he was called to go into the marketplace and preach the gospel with his life. Now his immersion is in the heart of God totally, and he enters into it and he begins the ascent of the mount of faith when he becomes one with Jesus Christ in Gethsemani, on the way of the cross, and at Golgotha. This is, as far as the pilgrim knows, the goal to which he is led.

Now the pilgrim who has heard the voice of him who was hidden in the burning bush knows what is in store. Now he has a choice. "Yes, or no. Yes, or no." So, because his faith has grown, and his love is passionate, his hope is assured, he follows. All along the line he follows. He doesn't know it but, I repeat again, a fire radiates from him. Not only a light, but a fire that the Lord sent to his heart. Why does the Lord send fire except to enkindle the hearts of men!

The pilgrim has become, in a sense, a torch. He is light and he is fire, and wherever he passes his footsteps remain. There is no need anymore to discuss with him the preaching of the gospel with his life. He is the gospel! He is fire and light. He is the icon of Christ. He is the gospel and he comes to the cross and meekly lies down.

At this point a miracle happens! The cross, the crown, the nails, the hammer—all disappear. The Lord embraces the pilgrim and says, "Well done, my friend. I tested you and you came through. I tested you to see what you could do with my help. And now you must begin the pilgrimage of daily reality. The pilgrimage of simplicity, docility, of true obedience, of chastity and poverty. All the gifts of the Holy Spirit are yours as are my heart and the blessing of my Father. Now, pilgrim, you are truly blessed, not only by your blood father and mother and the priests, but by Us. Now you can begin!"

7. Pilgrimaging in the Resurrected Christ

As THE LORD SAYS, now the pilgrim can begin.

In Russia a pilgrim is always blessed by his father and mother and parish priest before he sets off on his journey. It is not so everywhere, but it should be. The blessing of parents is a tremendous thing, but of course, so is the blessing of the Most Holy Trinity and of Our Lady!

Now the pilgrim begins in the fullness of the resurrected Christ. He has followed Christ through his Incarnation and his passion, and he was ready to be crucified. That's when he realized that Christ is with us and the miracle of his presence is the eternal miracle of the resurrection. He now functions, lives, has his being, breathes the resurrection.

But what is that reality that God calls forth from the pilgrim once he has entered its stream? This reality continues to be a love story between God and man. For his heart expands. A pilgrim has a heart that must encompass the world.

Do you realize exactly what the reality of pilgrimage is? Let us review it once more. The actual pilgrimage, in which a man leaves his home, his family, receives his blessings (if his parents are still alive) and conforms to the general image of what a pilgrim is, is one thing. But it is another thing to pilgrimage within oneself to meet the God that dwells within, and having met him to understand that from that moment the pilgrim does not belong to himself at all. It is a strange state of affairs, for a pilgrim can be anybody. I tried to explain in *Poustinia* that a pilgrim is a person who puts one foot in front of the other to traverse the world if necessary. Or he may not go very far from his home but fulfills the function of being a pilgrim. Or he may stand absolutely still.

Essentially, this latter function is first and foremost poverty, that strange kind of poverty that doesn't incline too drastically or hurriedly to changes of life. No, it is a poverty of the heart, the humble heart. Humility and poverty of the heart are twin companions of the pilgrim.

The pilgrim views everything he has and is as belonging to God and his brethren. There is a strange bookkeeping going on in his head: the least for himself; the most for others. His motto is "I am third": God, neighbor, myself. Yes, that's the strange reality of a pilgrimage in the resurrected Christ. It is so hard to explain how, after having become ready for crucifixion because of his love for God, one suddenly sees that that is not what God means. Consider Abraham. God holds the hand of Abraham so that Isaac his son is not hurt. So the pilgrim knows that God doesn't want him to be crucified in the reality of a cross and nails, but crucified in his will—the pilgrim's will—because of a passionate love of Christ that desires this strange crucifixion.

But what is this crucifixion? Why should a pilgrim experience this and not every Christian? Well, every Christian should—that is, have these propensities, these desires—but a pilgrim incarnates all these because he must walk as a gospel among his brethren.

The pilgrim in the resurrected Christ preaches the gospel without ceasing, night and day. He isn't only preaching it, he is living it. It is this pilgrimage of living the gospel day by day that a pilgrim embarks upon after he has passed the test and entered fully into the resurrection of

Jesus Christ. That is exactly what he has to do!

What does that mean in daily life to you and to me who are not experts in theology or spirituality or anything of that type, but whose hearts yearn to love God, to come closer to him, to be one with him? We know now that the only way to come closer to him is to come closer to our brethren, for if you say to your brother, "I want to touch God," all he has to reply is, "Touch me."

The reality of the pilgrimage in the resurrected Christ demands a surrender of one's will to God in a sort of totality. It demands that we do the most ordinary things, which the spiritual books call "the duty of the moment," for it is the duty of God. And all the time we pilgrimage to attend to the duty of the moment.

Let us analyze this a little. If you are a youth, the duty of the moment would probably be studying, going to school, doing your best in school, helping your parents in any way you can. It is walking in the midst of your peers unafraid, trusting that you are not going to say "yes" to anything that your peers might put forward that is not of God. Even if you are ostracized by your peers you still say a resounding "no," and because of this, in due time, they will understand that what you have done is to preach the gospel with your life. It is very difficult for a young one, a teenager, to defy peer opinion. If you love God and you realize that you have been called on a pilgrimage of preaching the gospel, that is what you are going to do.

The wife will attend to her duty of the moment, whatever it might be. Washing diapers and washing dishes, cooking and scrubbing and cleaning might be her lot, and she is not going to rebel against it because she is a pilgrim and she knows that she is only stopping in that house temporarily. God brought her there. Death will make her free, though she doesn't crave any kind of particular freedom because she has the immense freedom of the children of God in uniting her will to God's will.

Funny, isn't it, that the duty of the moment might be just scrubbing a floor? Of course, you may go to a psychiatrist and tell him your problem. If he finds out that your problem is anger, he will suggest that you scrub a floor because manual labor drains away the anger! But you are not going to do it because a psychiatrist tells you. You are not interested in the psychiatrist but in God's will. You are going to do it because it is the duty of the moment, because every moment is the moment of beginning again.

There is some kind of strange excitement and joy in doing things over and over and over again. The floor shines brighter. The windows are clearer. It's not only the floors that are shinier or the windows that are clearer: it is *you* that shines, resembling closer and closer the icon of Christ. And the people who see you, know you and talk to you, look through your eyes made clear and beautiful because they reflect God.

It is a strange pilgrimage that is only concerned with the duty of the moment and knows that every moment in God is the moment to begin again. Isn't that freeing and liberating!

Yes, the duty of the moment and the realization of every moment are the moment of beginning again. But there is more to it. It sounds drab and uninteresting presented this way, but it isn't. Again, it is the impossibility of explaining what happens to a pilgrim, who pilgrimages in the resurrected Christ, in the full realization that he is a pilgrim.

Now, back to what a pilgrim is. He is poor and he is humble of heart. His poverty is always covered with what the gospel calls "oiling one's hair," which is what they did in those days. What we mean by this is a very simple thing—that he dresses normally, that he appears not to be fasting, and yet he gives things away.

Perhaps a little story would help. I had a friend who was a fashion buyer for a big store. Twice a year she went to Europe, to Paris and other centers, to gather the latest fashions. She had a lovely apartment on 73rd Street in New York. It was filled with all kinds of knickknacks that she purchased on her trips abroad.

In her apartment was a hallway in which there was a huge cupboard full of every kind of dress for every occasion. She also had fine taste in costume jewelry. So as a handsome woman in her early 30's she really looked magnificent.

One day she went on a Dominican retreat. After the weekend she came out, called me up and said, "Catherine, I have to talk to you." (Whoever the good, holy Dominican retreat master was, he emphasized bourgeois living, the lack of poverty in the States, the lack of surrender to God's will, and so on. It made a profound impression on my friend.)

She said, "I am going to clean this place up," and she did. She gave away all the beautiful knickknacks to members of the department store, especially widows and people with families who could never afford such beautiful things.

She gave away most of her clothing to people her age, keeping a few dresses that she made over. She was an excellent seamstress and would show me how to change a dress just by putting a piece of lace or costume jewelry on it.

She redid her apartment, painting it gray. She had a red sofa bed and two red armchairs and explained that "I made them red so I will remember the wounds of Jesus Christ." The colors all matched very well.

She kept only one picture, a large and beautiful

picture of St. Francis. And that was all.

Then she opened her house. If anyone was lonely or recuperating from illness she would invite them in. She had an extra bedroom, so they shared her house with her. And all the time she was the best-dressed woman in that place, looking chic and smart. Nobody suspected her inner and deep poverty.

Well, a pilgrim who understands, who walks the inner road of poverty, also walks the road of fasting and praying. Again, nothing shows on the outside. Especially in our time of diets, it's so easy to say, "I am on a diet" and not add, "a diet for God and man." That's the road the pilgrim walks who is in the resurrected Christ. For if he is to be the gospel and to preach it both with his words and with his being, he will have to pray constantly, and serve constantly, and fast constantly.

Then comes another road the pilgrim has to face. It's the road of "pleasure." Obviously the pilgrim is not going to indulge even in many legitimate pleasures, like smoking, for instance. Smoking is injurious to health, but that is not the main point for the pilgrim. What is important is giving in to desires not blessed by God.

The pilgrim has to walk on the road of self-denial. He has to walk the road of self-discipline. Smoking, sex out of marriage, liquor, gambling—all these cravings need to be controlled. Like Matt Talbot, we realize that the pilgrim walks the road of self-discipline and surrender of pleasures because he loves God. This does not mean that pilgrims don't marry. It doesn't mean that they don't drink occasionally. It doesn't mean that they don't play bingo. No. It means that the self-discipline is deep and profound because the pilgrim sees the road he has to travel. He knows that it is the road of Christ and he knows that he must be free to travel it, and that these so-called "passions," as they were called in the old spiritual books, restrain and crush him.

In the resurrected Christ the pilgrim has to do all these things. But that is only the beginning.

His poverty must bear fruit. It bears fruit in his giving away all the surplus he has, and whenever possible he gives of his necessities.

His fasting is not only for himself. As all gifts of God, it is for others, to atone for all those who give in to all kinds of excesses, be it drinking, smoking, or eating. Yes, he understands now very clearly his role in helping Christ.

Poverty and humility of heart keep him walking those paths. But there is still obedience. The pilgrim is obedient unto death because he has been led to a cross, and he has surrendered his life. For one split second of his life he has surrendered and been ready to be crucified. But the Lord took away this pain, though he didn't take away the memory of it, and the pilgrim has to walk the road of obedience because the God he loves was obedient unto death. There is no way out.

To whom shall he be obedient, this pilgrim? To the authorities of the Church, to those who have a right to his obedience, be it the boss of a department store, or a doctor, a superintendent, anyone who is over him. He has to be obedient to the laws of his country and he has to be obedient to the laws of all countries if he encounters them.

But above all he has to be obedient to that inner voice of his conscience that eternally tells him what is right and what is wrong. The inner voice of his conscience which, of course, is always checked by his spiritual director or in confession. It is humbling to be eternally obedient, but that's what God wants so that man does not do what he wants but what God wants. A pilgrim above all has to be close to his spiritual director and be obedient to him.

I have a little story. I was a salesclerk in a department store and I was making quite a lot of commissions. I was, in fact, making the highest commissions in the department store. Whereas the salary was only $12.50, the commission was twice as big. So the personnel manager called me in and he said, "How is it that you are such a good salesclerk?"

I said, "Well, nothing special happens. I like selling, but that's not the point. The point is that I made a contract with your company to be on the job eight hours a day. There is my lunch hour, and there are moments when I have to depart from the floor—nature calls! But I consider all the rest of it is yours. I do not consider it is time to talk to the other salesclerks or to go and powder my nose again and again. That's not my idea. I consider a contract is a moral affair, the more so because I made it also with God."

Well, I must admit that the personnel manager swallowed twice and he said, "Pardon me?" I said, "You see, any contract that any person enters into has a moral connotation and anything that is moral has something to do with God too."

"Hmmm, hmmm," he mused, "I don't think that you can explain that to our salesclerks, can you? I was hoping that you could give a lecture on it." "Oh no," I said, "probably I could, but it would be a little difficult."

Now here is the picture that I am trying to present of a pilgrim. A pilgrim knows that he has to walk on this road of obedience to his superiors, whoever they are. So I had a moral obligation to spend eight hours a day selling. If I didn't want to sell, I could quit, but I couldn't fritter away the time, for this would be wrong. The pilgrim knows this as he walks that road of moral obligation which is, after all, the duty of the moment. My duty was selling.

8. The Heartbeats of God

I HAVE TRIED TO EXPLAIN what a pilgrimage is as I see it with my Russian eyes. But do you know something? I really haven't said very much, have I? At least my heart tells me that there is much more to say, and I am wondering what it is that my heart tells me.

I have an idea that the best way to find things out is to rest upon Christ's breast, like St. John did, and hear his heartbeats. Somehow, hearing the heartbeats of God clarifies everything. And then again, it clarifies nothing except to lead you into a mystery beyond reckoning.

Yet, as I try to share with you what to me is a pilgrimage, I come to that mystery of Christ's heart and I know that I haven't yet finished it, because the mysteries of God are very strange. There are moments when he lifts a corner of the veil of his mystery and allows you to see one part, one little part of it. For a moment the view stops your senses and you lose all contact with yourself and everybody else. But it's only for a moment, because when God reveals his mysteries, even a little of them, he does so that those who have seen them might pass them on to others. Of course, there is an immense mystery in that pilgrimage that I am trying to tell you about. I have studied theology and philosophy and have found, over a period of long years, that they are like dust in my mouth.

I agree with St. Thomas Aquinas: he wanted to burn his writings once he beheld God. He was praying before a crucifix and suddenly saw the arm of God—a wooden arm—reach down and touch him. After this he didn't even want to read what he had written. His innumerable theses that we all study seemed like dust to him.

There are many books on theology. Some of them should never have been written! Some of them are beautiful. But, my friends, the pilgrim gets his knowledge directly from the heartbeats of God, from the veil that God deigns to lift to allow the pilgrim to behold a tiny part of God's own mystery. That is where the pilgrim really learns the science of God. Actually, it is the science about God, but when God becomes the teacher it becomes the science of God. Only God can explain himself.

So the pilgrim comes to a point where he has to rest, not in the depths of men's hearts, but in the heart of God. He has to listen to the heartbeats of God and he has to become "suspended," as it were. The Lord in his immense goodness and mercy lifts a little corner of his own mystery so that the pilgrim can really preach him in the marketplace, so that he really can become a gospel, so that he really can become fire and flame, fire and light!

Strange as it might seem, this process, this encounter, this revelation of God to the pilgrim, may take quite a while.

The pilgrim continues to be and do what God asked him to do: preach the gospel in the marketplace. But something new has been added to him. While he preaches by his life, his words and his presence, and while the windows of his eyes become almost totally transparent so that men can see God reflected in them, at the same time the pilgrim is taken up by the Wind!

It might be a tornado. It might be a very powerful

wind. It might be a breeze. That is up to God. But it is to be remembered that, while the pilgrim himself is taken up by the Wind, he never ceases to be available, to be at the service of everyone, to be in fact what he should be: a living gospel in the marketplace.

But now God has decided to really bring him high up on the mountain of faith. That requires a wind to get him there, the wind of the Spirit. The pilgrim ceases to be a novice. He enters into God's friendship, for the Lord says to him, "I shall not call you servants anymore, because a servant does not know his master's business; I call you friends because I have made known to you everything I have learned from my Father."

The gifts of the Spirit are beginning to be more clearly defined in the pilgrim.

Maybe in the Wind he will receive the gift of prophecy, of healing, of discernment—one of the seven gifts or more. No one can tell because the pilgrim is entering an entirely new aspect of his pilgrimage!

Accustomed as he is by now to doing the will of God —passionately desirous of doing it—he is awed nevertheless that he has been called to so strange a pilgrimage, totally human, and strangely divine. But then, of course, it is said in the scriptures, "In making these gifts, he has given us the guarantee of something very great and wonderful to come: through them you will be able to share the divine nature and to escape corruption in a world that is sunk in vice" (2 Pt 1:4). And so I face my heart and I begin to realize that more has to be written about pilgrims and pilgrimages. There is a whole other aspect to it.

In the West they would call this "mystical." If you want to use the word "mystical" for "mystery," call it "mystical." All contacts with God and man are mystical, but it doesn't appear to me to be anything mystical. To me it is simply God's mercy and God's love encompassing me and you and all the other pilgrims, and lifting us up high, high, high onto the mountain of faith.

One must never forget, though, that everything that happens to a Christian, all the gifts given to him by God from his baptism in the death and resurrection of Christ, makes him part of Christ's body of which Christ is the head. From that moment on, everything he receives is for *others*. At no time is any gift of the Holy Spirit or any gift of the Trinity for himself. Always, always it must be for others, and in that strange communion, in that strange situation lies the *kenosis* of the pilgrim and of the Christian who is such a pilgrim.

Having given everything away like all pilgrims should and must, he now is faced with gifts that are showered on him through the Wind, through the heart of the Trinity. And now begins the temptation of the pilgrim. His hands slowly form themselves into fists so that he can hold onto the gifts for himself. This is one of the most subtle temptations that the devil can produce.

The gifts showered by the Spirit, by the Wind, by the Trinity, that bring us up almost to the summit of faith, are known to Lucifer. He arises out of his depths to come and tempt the pilgrim with *virtue*. The devil tempts by virtue too. He whispers to the pilgrim as if he, Lucifer, were part of the Wind, but he can blow too and the pilgrim might not hear too well. Lucifer says to the pilgrim: "Look! Don't you see you are being given the gift of healing? Isn't that wonderful? You are going to heal the people! Thousands will come to you. Perhaps more than thousands. You will be able to help everybody . . . everybody! See how the Wind is about to give you that gift of healing."

The pilgrim must stop. In the very Wind of the Spirit and the embrace of the Trinity the pilgrim must stop and pray, crying out to God, "Help me to get rid of the Tempter!" He has to, because he might listen. Lucifer can imitate the Wind for a second or two. One can make a mistake, can falter. If the hand of the pilgrim clutches onto the gift of healing because he thinks he can do it by himself, or because he thinks that God means it for himself, suddenly he can fall back from the mountain of faith. He doesn't hear the real Wind anymore, and a total darkness envelops him. These are the moments when one must stay close to one's spiritual director. One must stay close to God. These are the moments when our Lady comes to the forefront of the pilgrim's life because God promised that her heel would crush the voice of the Tempter, even the Tempter himself.

Yes, the pilgrim has entered another phase. He has become the friend of God. He has also opened himself to being tempted as Jesus Christ was tempted. All this knowledge, all this beauty, and even the breath of evil that is trying to come in—God permitted all this so that the pilgrim might bring the gifts of God back to the marketplace. In his cupped and open palms he brings them back, totally immune to any false humility, to presumption, to any of those (shall we call them) "situations" that can arise. He is totally immune to them. The pilgrim doesn't change. He stands in the marketplace radiating more and more fire, but he doesn't know it. He is steeped in joy, humility of heart, and docility. And the strangest thing happens when he returns from these ways of God: he becomes a child.

True, he preaches the gospel with his life, but now people know that he belongs to Bethlehem and Nazareth. People know that he has the heart of a child. And his prayer is, "Lord, give me the heart of a child and the courage to live it out." But already God has given him the courage to do so and he lives it out in the marketplace.

The impact of his life is fantastic, for now he constantly reproduces in his life the Incarnation, the preaching, the suffering, the death, and the resurrection of the Lord!

Do you see what my heart told me?